GRANT ME THE SERENITY

TO ACCEPT THE THINGS
I CANNOT CHANGE,
THE COURAGE TO CHANGE
THE THINGS I CAN, AND
THE WISDOM TO KNOW
THE DIFFERENCE.

-NIEBUHR-

Serenity

Courage   Wisdom

P C T

Prayer Changes Things

Copyright © 2021 by Santiego Rivers

All rights reserved. This book may not be reproduced or transmitted in any form without the written permission of the author.

"no copyright infringement is intended."

ISBN 978-1-7376037-0-2

To learn to stand and square up like a man, I first had to go down to my knees and learn how to pray like a child.

> "Train up a child in the way he should go: and when he is old, he will not depart from it." -**Proverb 22:6**

God raised me from the ashes, so I am still humbly serving and praising my creator today.

Respectfully, I admit that I am not a religious person, but I am a spiritual being who will always give praise to the Most High.

> "Great is thy faith be it unto thee "
> **Matthew 9:29 KJV**

My creator has delivered me from the valley to the mountain tops just so that I can go down on my knees and say thank you.

Thank you for the blessings that I can see in my life.

Thank you for all the prayers that have yet to manifest into my life.

I want to say thank you for giving my life purpose and meaning.

I may have struggled to get back on the path that he had for me in my life, but my creator never left my side when the people I depended on turned their back on me.

I serve an awesome creator!

Other people wanted to hold me to my past indiscretions; my creator saw the potential in me and my willingness to combine my **faith** and **hard work** to become the best version of myself and stayed by my side.

Prayer Changes Things

I had to learn how to pray and the power that comes from praying before I overstood that I only needed to *meditate* because my creator already knows what I **need** in my life.

Prayer Changes Things

I used my prayer as a way of opening my hearts to the Most High and humbling myself to his will and not my own desire.

When you pray from your heart, you tap into your authentic self. You tap into your spirit as a spiritual being.

When you go down on your knees and pray, you remove pride from your path and put your life in a different direction. Doing this will lead you to your salvation.

Prayer Changes Things

The most amazing thing about prayer is that it allows you to give your problems to the Most High and let them go.

Worrying about something will never make anything better in your life. **Let it go**!

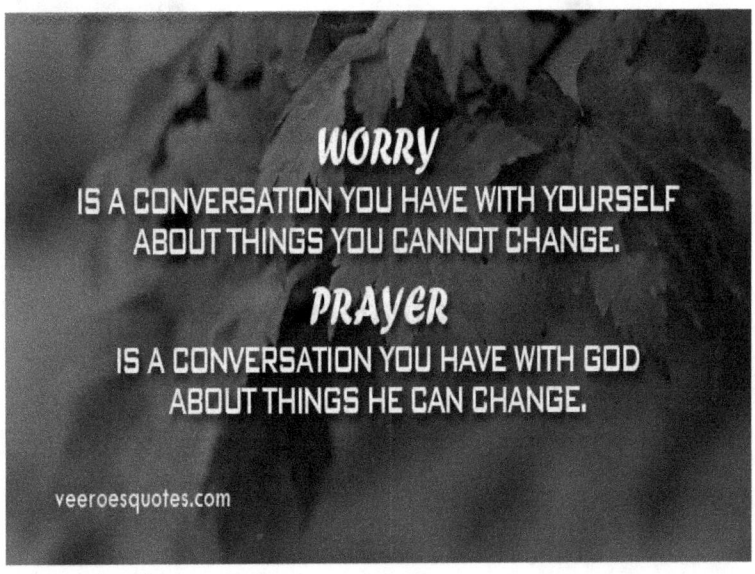

Won't he do it!

God is good **(all the time)**

All the time **(God is good)**

Sometimes you have to encourage yourself because if you don't learn to do it for yourself, no one else ever will.

Prayer Changes Things

Prayers do not change God's mind; He ordains prayer as a means to accomplish His will for our benefit.

I remember times in my life that I wanted to forget those bad times in my life, but praying about it taught me that if I didn't go through those tough times in my life, I would not have the strength to go down on my knees and give my worries to God.

Prayer Changes Things

I thought that I was a strong person both mentally and physically, but prayer taught me what true strength was and will always be.

Prayer Changes Things

How can something so humbling be so mighty and so fulfilling? I don't have the answer to this question, but I do know that prayer provides all these things and more.

Prayer Changes Things

I remember my grandmother always praying over my brother as a child and me. So today, I seek her prayers when my life is getting too much to bear.

Prayer has and is still changing things

She taught me that prayer could move mountains and part the seas if you are strong enough to put your faith in prayer.

Prayer Changes Things

My grandmother was and is my Moses, my Noah, and everything important to me. If you like the man I am today, you have to love the woman who helped make all of this possible. **(I am still a work in progress)**

I had a severe eye injury as a child, which caused my left eyelid not to open. The doctors thought that I would never be able to open or see anything out of that eye again. So I had to wear an eye patch.

My grandmother is the type of person who has always felt that no matter what man says, take your problems to God and see what he does.

She prayed over me before I went to school each day, and she showed me that only God should and will have the say-so over my life. As a result, my eye opened one day when I came home from school, and I have sight out of it still today.

Prayer Changes Things

My faith was grounded in prayer early as a child, so it is easy for me to keep prayer in my life today. I encourage anyone I speak with to try prayer out, especially when your way of doing things is not working.

Prayer Changes Things

I don't know about you, but for me, if I tried to accomplish half of the things that I try to do on my own, I would surely fail.

Believe me; I have tried, failed, and tried again, which lead me to quit many things in my life.

I was and unfortunately still am, in some ways, a stubborn person, but when I have to go down on my knees and pray, I surely do.

Prayer Changes Thing

- Pride?
- What pride?
- Embarrassment?
- What embarrassment?

There is no shame in me when it comes to knowing and understanding the power that prayer has in my life.

This is my life without prayer:

This is my life with prayer:

Hopefully, you can see why I am going to stick with praying faithfully because I have learned. **Prayer Changes Things**

When I feel misunderstood, scrutinized, betrayed, overwhelmed, and all of those things God did not create me to be:

I pray

When my mind won't stop overthinking, and my fears and worries are getting the best of me:

I pray

I give all of my problems to God and trust what he has consistently shown me in the past. He will always deliver.

This is why I pray

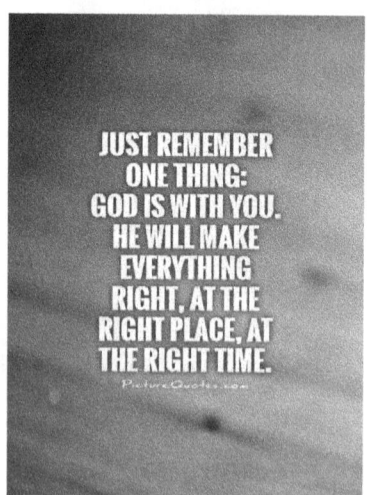

Prayer teaches the virtues of **patience** and **dedication**. I can't tell you how many times I went down on my knees to pray about something and before I could make it to my feet, I was trying to handle the problem myself.

I am sure that you can imagine how it turned out for me in the end. I had to go back to my knees and give my problems and worries back to God.

Remember I told you that I was a stubborn person, so this process happened numerous times. That is me putting it mildly.

I lost a few pounds and messed up my knees, going up and down so much to pray.

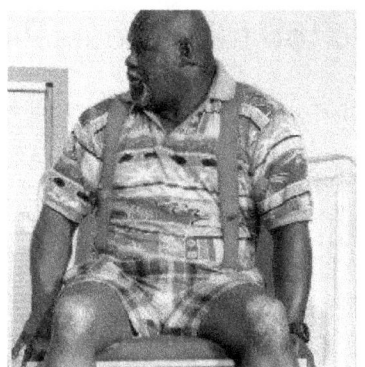

I know God must be tired of hearing from me after all these years?

Once you learn that prayer changes things, why would you not want to pray?

- Are you too prideful?
- Are you too stubborn?
- Are you too full of yourself?

I wonder would God allow me to have your blessings since you don't want yours?

It is just a thought! I was just joking! Unless he will let me have them? I'll do some extra praying! **I know that prayer Changes Things**

When is the right time to pray? Well, let me tell you again when I pray.

When I feel that the world around me is against me,

I pray

When I feel the presence of evil around me,
I pray.

When it feels like the walls are closing in on me,

I pray.

When things are going well in my life, **I pray.**

When I find a reason to smile and be happy,
I pray.

Even when I can't remember when was the last time I prayed, I begin to **pray.**

Prayer Changes Things, which is why I constantly pray

Pride comes before the fall, so you might as well go to your knees and pray while you are down there.

A man stands tallest when he is on his knees

I do my best work from my knees. Take that how you want to, but the results speak for themselves.

Words have power and meaning, which is why my words needed to be filled with both meaning and purpose as I learned how to pray.

I have learned many prayers in my life, but the one that is my rock is the serenity prayer.

Serenity Prayer

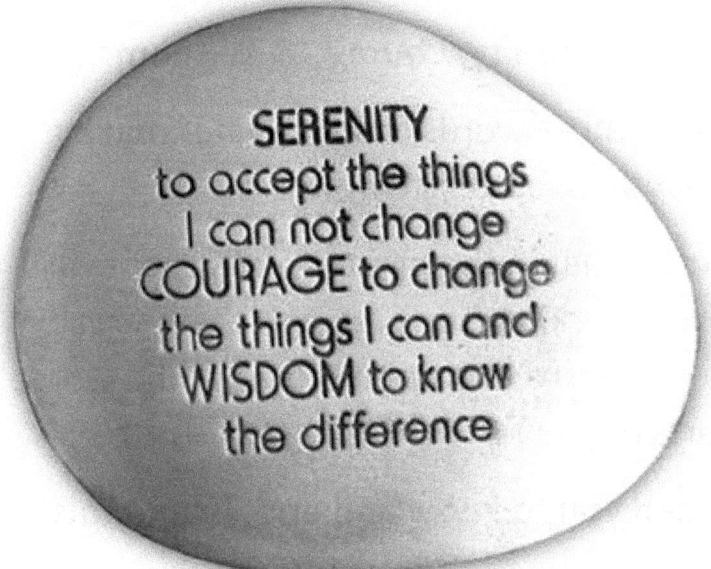

The Serenity Prayer is my rock that keeps me on course when the devil tries to change my path.

Serenity, Courage,& Wisdom

Serenity, Courage, and **Wisdom** are the base of my foundation. Without Knowledge, understanding, and acceptance of those things, I would be lost in the wilderness.

Serenity, Courage,& Wisdom

Those three words *change things* making everything better in my life.

I know that in the presence of good, evil is always lurking. The enemy is always ready to give you a reason to bring out the worse parts of you.

I need you to know and understand this!

The enemy is not fighting you because you are weak. On the contrary, the enemy knows the power and strength within you even when you deny your greatness.

If it were not for the challenges we face in our lives, we would never know how strong we really are.

Embrace the person you want to be, and don't allow anyone to hold you to the person you used to be.

If you understand that prayer changes things, why can't it change you?

They have taken prayer out of school, which is why we must arm our kids with the armor of God before we send them out into the belly of the beast.

Personally, I do not want to be anywhere where I cant serve and worship my God, but to reach those in need, you must travel outside of your comfort zone.

To Karen & Bill

If you only knew how much my God was helping me to be a calmer and understanding being, you would thank my God yourself.

Please remember that he is still working on me, and I do have a past that I am trying to leave behind me.

Would you please not take my kindness for a weakness and make me explain the *Art of War* to you?

Appear weak when you are strong, and strong when you are weak – **Sun Tzu**

Let my smile remind you that although prayer does change things, The Most High is not done working on me yet.

I still have those rough edges that need to be smooth out.

Please pray for me!

What things in your life do you need God to help you with to become the best version of yourself?

www.ingramcontent.com/pod-product-compliance
Lightning Source LLC
Chambersburg PA
CBHW071014160426
43193CB00012B/2051